GET THAT PROMOTION

Based on *Getting On* by Joanna Gaudoin

First published in Great Britain by Practical Inspiration Publishing, 2025

ISBN   978-1-78860-812-1   (paperback)
          978-1-78860-813-8   (ebook)

EU GPSR representative: LOGOS EUROPE, 9 rue Nicolas Poussin, LA ROCHELLE 17000, France Contact@ logoseurope.eu.

Want to bulk-buy copies of this book for your team and colleagues? We can customize the content and co-brand *Get That Promotion* to suit your business's needs.

Please email info@practicalinspiration.com for more details.

Practical Inspiration Publishing™

Contents

Series introduction

Welcome to *6-Minute Smarts*!

This is a series of very short books with one simple purpose: to introduce you to ideas that can make life and work better, and to give you time and space to think about how those ideas might apply to *your* life and work.

Each book introduces you to ten powerful ideas, but ideas on their own are useless – that's why each idea is followed by self-coaching questions to help you work out the 'so what?' for you in just six minutes of exploratory writing. What's exploratory writing? It's the kind of writing you do just for yourself, fast and free, without worrying what anyone else thinks. It's not just about getting ideas out of your head and onto paper where you can see them; it's about finding new connections and insights as you write. This is where the magic happens.

Whatever you're facing, there's a *6-Minute Smarts* book just for you. Once you've learned how to coach yourself through a new idea, you'll be smarter for life.

Find out more...

Introduction

Where are you in your career right now? Have you got to where you wanted? Perhaps you feel you've made good progress but have come up against a challenge. Or maybe you're feeling frustrated, annoyed, despondent, in a rut – or simply wanting to look ahead and make the most of your working life. Or it could be that you've been passed over for the next promotion, and you've identified some development areas you need to tackle to take you to the next level.

This book is for you if you feel you've had a good career so far but you're now encountering some challenges in your day-to-day work or barriers to moving forward, or if you simply want to look ahead and think about the skills you need so you can really achieve all you want to at work.

You spend an enormous amount of time at work and it's likely to be a key part of your identity. Therefore, taking the time to make it as enjoyable and successful as you can (whatever that means for you) is worthwhile.

Wherever you are at in your working life, I hope this book will be a catalyst to enable you to navigate your challenges more easily so your working days will become more fulfilling and your career can move forward.

Most people I have worked with over the last decade or so have had successful careers. At the point when they choose to work with me, they are generally facing a specific challenge, know things aren't how they would like (although they may not know exactly why) or realize they need to broaden their skillset to continue their progression and gain a greater sense of fulfilment. This book incorporates much of the guidance I have offered to clients over time and includes some anonymous mini case studies to bring this guidance to life.

This book is about helping you to become aware of the skills you need. They may not be new to you, but if you haven't implemented them then you won't have benefited. This book is highly practical, explaining the why as well as the what and the how, so you can take action.

Introduction

The big challenge is that most people focus predominantly on their technical skills and knowledge. This is unsurprising if you consider the usual emphasis on gaining knowledge through education to secure your first job.

But technical skills and knowledge on their own are insufficient as you progress in your career. You also need to work on your non-technical – dare I say 'soft' – skills too, to stand out from other people with excellent technical skills. Also, as artificial intelligence becomes more widely used, the people who will succeed will be those who have developed their non-technical skills – the skills a computer can't readily replicate.

Even if you DO get promoted based on your technical knowledge and skills, they won't be enough to help you succeed in your new role. The day job changes with seniority.

The sooner you can become aware of this challenge and work on the necessary skills presented in this book, the better you'll be able to weather the inevitable storms and achieve greater fulfilment in your career.

Other people are almost always at the heart of the challenges you will face at work, whether it's a perceived personality clash, a lack of recognition, a lack of support or difficulty getting your voice heard.

That is why everything in this book relates to how you show up at work and engage with others, in different professional scenarios.

Most of what is covered in this book involves an investment of time, and often conscious behavioural change. In most instances, there are no 'quick fixes' but by starting to work on what I cover and taking small steps, you can make significant progress.

Before you start, I strongly suggest you take a step back and do a brief SWOT (Strengths, Weaknesses, Opportunities and Threats) analysis of your career so you can identify the areas you need to focus on. If you do that, it will help you to be more focused as you read this book.

Make some notes, use some page markers, do whatever you need to do to highlight the elements that are relevant to you so you can come back to them and plan.

Remember how much you have achieved. Everything in this book is to help you move forward from wherever you are at and build your confidence rather than dent it.

Day 1
Understanding personal impact

You walk into a room... You receive an email... You answer your phone... In those initial moments, you think something about the person or people you encounter. They also think something about you.

Humans continually form perceptions of others. It's the way your brain protects you: by taking what it has experienced and learned and using that to inform you about the people you encounter.

That's why your personal impact is so important and why you need to consider it wherever and whenever you encounter others – especially in a professional context.

Not only does it affect how you are perceived by others, but it also affects how confident you feel about yourself.

First impressions are made quickly – some research suggests a tenth of a second, others say two, five or even seven seconds.[1] It's impossible for you to communicate nothing about yourself when you encounter someone else.

Harvard Research says it takes up to eight positive things to reverse a negative first impression back to neutral. So why make it hard for yourself?

You can't entirely control others' perceptions. How they perceive the world is affected by their upbringing, their values and their experiences, among other elements. However, you can carefully consider what you project to others by developing awareness and considering how you engage.

How people form perceptions and impressions

One theory I find really helpful here is *strength and warmth*, which is set out brilliantly in John Neffinger and Matthew Kohut's book *Compelling People*.[2] When people meet, they subconsciously assess how competent someone appears to be and how trustworthy and friendly they seem.

Strength is about appearing confident and capable – upright posture, eye contact, dressing appropriately.

Warmth is about friendliness – smiling and an open, engaged body position. When meeting someone for the first time, warmth matters most. Without warmth, others will struggle to engage and may even shut themselves off from you if it feels risky to start an interaction. The reason why warmth matters so much is because, as much as we may sometimes not like to acknowledge it, we are emotional as well as logical beings. (But don't overdo it: warmth without strength can be just as off-putting as strength without warmth!)

Remember that, while generally a balance of strength and warmth is beneficial, in certain situations a different balance is necessary. If one of your team is under-performing, in an initial discussion you may increase your warmth to try to understand, to get them to talk about the situation and make it clear that you want to help them. However, if you end up having the same discussion a third or fourth time, more strength is likely to be called for.

It might be helpful to consider more senior people who you think have a positive impact; what is it about them and how they engage with others that's so effective?

Your personal brand

First impressions are important, particularly in situations where people don't have long to make a decision about you or you about them (interviews and pitch meetings, for example). However, in many professional contexts, it is about so much more. It is about how you continually build on the (hopefully) positive first impression to develop your personal brand.

Most of us are familiar with the concept of brand when it comes to the things we buy – clothes, shoes, household items, food, cars, etc. When you think about it, what this really means is that you have associations with certain brands. This assumes the brand has done a good enough job of defining what it is about and then communicating it. It means you often decide quickly whether or not a brand is for you.

When you think about *your* personal brand, consider what the colleague who knows you well would say about you to the person who knows you less well once you have left the meeting room. What picture is being painted of you? Do you know how others perceive you and how they would describe you?

A good way to summarize your personal brand is to consider which three words (not technical skills) best represent you. These words should be positive adjectives and be realistic about who you are, yet also a little aspirational (you can find a personal brand reflection sheet that can help with this on my website).[3] Keep these words at the front of your mind when you are making decisions and taking action. Ask yourself, 'Does this support my brand?' If not, that may be fine if there's a good business reason for it, but very often this thinking can help you stay on track.

A clear personal brand helps you to focus and consider how you come across to others. It needs to be authentic and genuine, yet appropriate for your professional context. When you have a personal brand that is based on these attributes, you will feel energized and it will affect how others react to you. It's definitely not about being someone else but rather being the best possible version of yourself.

How you show up in every scenario at work matters – your personal impact matters a great deal and is foundational to the relationships you build, the influence you have and ultimately your career success.

So what? Over to you...

1. How might you be perceived on a good day versus a stressful or tiring one?

2. What three words would you want others to use to describe your personal brand?

3. How could you start being more intentional about the impact you make in your day-to-day interactions?

Day 2
Dressing for career success

Your appearance has a huge effect on your personal impact.

It might sound superficial; after all, why should what you wear matter? Surely doing your job well is enough?

However, your clothing heavily influences the impression you transmit. Mary Lynn Damhorst, a leading researcher in apparel, determined in 1990 that in studies, 81% said that dress communicated someone's competence, power and intelligence, while nearly 67% said it also communicated character, sociability and mood.[4] Your choice of clothing can heavily influence the impression you transmit.

Forty years ago, the lines were clearer – in a professional office environment, everyone would

13

have been wearing suits and, in the case of men, ties. It made it easy, if dull, to get dressed for work every day. These days we have greater flexibility and choice, more opportunity to bring in our personality and more ways to be memorable.

The golden rule now is 'appropriateness'. What you wear each day depends on whether you're in the office, who you're meeting and what will help you to perform to the best of your abilities.

Dressing appropriately for your day

Always consider your plans for the day and the people you are likely to encounter to help you decide what impact you need and want to make.

It's worth keeping some principles in mind that relate broadly to how authoritative versus how approachable you want to appear. It's not all or nothing, though; usually it's a blend of the two.

If you need to look more authoritative, wear neutrals like black, navy or white, combine very dark and very light clothing, and choose structured, plain clothing, avoiding patterns or details.

To come across as more approachable, the opposite choices help: more interesting colours (though always teamed with at least one neutral), less structured clothing, more patterns.

You can combine elements from both authoritative and approachable dressing to meet the demands of your day, remembering that sometimes meetings are unplanned. If your office dress code is more relaxed, it's worth considering what you can keep at the office to smarten up an outfit – a jacket, scarf or different shoes.

Clothing choices that work for you

It's not just about what others think; it's about you too. Think about what makes you feel and look good.

Wearing what suits you physically is also important. The key considerations are the shape and fit of clothing and the colour. Next time you're at the shops looking for clothing, try something different. Pick out some clothing of very different colours, such as dark/light and brighter/more muted, then put them up to your face. You will see that some work better than others. If you trust the shop assistant, ask their opinion too. Think about context too: if you want to be seen easily – such as when speaking at an event or in a large online meeting – a statement colour is a good choice; if you want to be seen as authoritative, then go for neutrals.

Check that clothes fit you well, with no pulling or gaping, and that they are the right shape for you. (So, not the shirt you wore when you were 6kg lighter or heavier!)

Ill-fitting clothes that draw attention to the wrong parts of you can be uncomfortable and distracting for you and others – especially if you spend half the meeting pulling an item of clothing back into place.

Take time to look at your wardrobe and discard anything that looks worn out, doesn't fit or doesn't make you feel good.

As you aim at promotion and more senior levels, having a unique personal style can help you be more memorable. Take some time to consider what that might be – look for inspiration in shops, online and in magazines, if that will help. It doesn't mean you have to always wear the same outfit in a different colour or the same colour, but rather that you develop a style that suits you, and that works for you and your professional life.

You never want your clothes to be the main focus, but if you get your dress right for what the other person expects in a given situation – the sector in which they work, the type of meeting, where you are meeting and your role – they are more likely to focus on what you say.

Of course, appearance is just part of the visual impact you have. Next we're going to look at another extremely important visual aspect: body language.

So what? Over to you...

1. What message do your usual work clothes send about you, and is that the message you want to send?

2. What adjustments could you make to help your appearance align more closely with your personal brand?

3. How can you better plan your outfit choices to match the needs of your working day?

Day 3
Mastering body language at work

A twitch of the lip... A raised eyebrow... A shuffle in your chair... even when you're not speaking, if someone else can see you, you're communicating. Research shows most human communication takes place through body language. You also get clues about others' thoughts and feelings from theirs.

Beware of over-interpreting single cues like crossed arms, which could indicate defensiveness – or simply that someone is cold. You need to read the whole person, not just one signal.

It's easier to read body language when you know someone well. You'll spot what's different. With new people, it's harder – you don't know their 'norm'.

But in any case, be careful – it's very easy to read body language incorrectly and much depends on cultural context. This book is based on a western perspective, although, of course, there are some cultural nuances within that sweeping area of geography.

We've already thought about the importance of consistency regarding your personal brand and how you deal with others. This also applies to what your body language is saying and what you're saying out loud. If your body language and your words contradict, it's the body language people believe – consciously or not. You don't have to 'lie' to send mixed signals; uncertainty, stress or discomfort can show through in small, involuntary ways.

That's why it's important to manage how you present yourself physically, particularly in high-stakes conversations, and that's why this chapter is all about using body language for personal impact and engaging more effectively with others.

The key body language elements to consider

Whole books much bigger than this one have been written about body language. Here I'm just going to outline the key aspects that I have seen really make a difference for my clients over the years. (NB you can download a useful body language elements worksheet from my website to help with this section.[5])

Posture: Posture is particularly important because – unlike facial expressions, say – it's visible from a distance. A more erect posture, whether seated or standing, communicates increased confidence and credibility. Slouching suggests lack of confidence or low energy.

Movement: Movement should be deliberate. Moving at a relatively quick pace may make you appear dynamic, focused and confident, but if it isn't definite it can simply look anxious. Too-fast movement can also appear stressed or impatient, especially to junior colleagues. If you're managing others, constantly rushing may make you seem unapproachable – even if that's not your intention. But you can also go too far the other way – inappropriate slowness can communicate reticence and lack of confidence.

Owning your space: Making yourself smaller – crossing arms or legs, slouching, pulling limbs inward – can come across as lacking confidence. Confident people appear more 'settled' in their space. This changes depending on context. Presenting? Take up more space. Fielding questions? Soften slightly. As always, context is king.

Smiling: In western culture, smiling is a great professional ice breaker. It helps to communicate warmth, but it also needs to be appropriate. One client of mine smiled constantly during a mock interview, and it affected his credibility. People can become suspicious that a fixed smile isn't genuine, and it may even become be a distraction.

Eye contact: We've all met someone who avoids or can't sustain eye contact, so you already know how disconcerting and awkward this can be. When we look into someone else's eyes, we feel more connected and engage more effectively. Aim to look people in the eye around 50–70% of the time in a one-on-one conversation. Lack of eye contact can make you seem disengaged – or even untrustworthy. And, obviously, avoid looking at your phone mid-conversation unless clearly necessary. If you're presenting, then looking around the room and attempting to make eye contact is essential to keep people engaged.

Hand gestures: Do you use hand gestures? You probably don't know, as they're so instinctive. Next time you're explaining something in a meeting or a presentation, try to notice what you're doing with your hands. It can be challenging to know what to do with hands, especially when you're nervous. But don't just sit on them.

Gestures increase impact. They help you take up space, reinforce your points and signal confidence. Gestures should be deliberate – not twitchy or erratic. Try moving a hand from left to right across your body to show the progression of an argument, or to tick off points on your fingers as you make them. Avoid going above your shoulders, which can come across as aggressive, or rushing others with impatient movements.

Facial expressions: Facial expressions reflect your emotions, so you need to be particularly aware of them and the impact they can have on others, especially during sensitive conversations. Try not to show disagreement or confusion too early when listening. Learn to manage your 'resting face' too – it may signal boredom or irritation when that's not how you feel.

Some expressions are almost involuntary; it's hard to have command over micro gestures such as blushing or a mouth twitch, but it can be helpful to observe them in others. After all, if the key person you need to influence in a meeting is showing signs of disengagement or disagreement, being able to deal with that is essential.

A note about virtual body language

In virtual settings, body language is harder to read – but still critical. Fidgeting is amplified. Avoid only showing your head – include your hands if you can. Sit still, grounded in your chair. Look at the camera now and then to simulate eye contact. Remember that mirroring still works over video – adopt a similar seated posture to others to help build rapport.

Remember how effective body language is when it comes to reading others and to changing what you want to convey, whether that be credibility through stillness or excitement/passion through quicker yet still deliberate movements and expressions.

So what? Over to you…

1. What aspects of your body language may be unintentionally undermining your confidence or credibility?

2. How does your posture or eye contact change in meetings with senior colleagues versus peers or direct reports?

3. Which non-verbal signals could you manage more intentionally in your next high-stakes interaction?

Day 4

The art of effective communication

A pause... A shift in tone... A slight rise in pitch – how you say something can completely change how it's received. This is especially true when you're not visible, like on a phone call.

How you speak matters

Let's explore in more detail why your voice matters and what you need to consider in order to make the right impression with it.

Volume: You need to be heard. Speaking too quietly can send a message that you don't feel confident about what you are saying – that you don't think it deserves to be heard. If you don't think it's important, then why should others? It might mean you're literally not heard. If they didn't catch what you said people will only ask you to repeat it once or twice because asking more than that makes them feel stupid or rude. Volume also supports confidence. If you tend to be quiet, work on deeper breathing; the more breath you have behind your voice, the more power/volume it will have.

Pace: The most common issue I see amongst my clients – even the most senior ones – is speaking too fast. They forget that while what they are saying is familiar to them, in most cases it's new to the people they're talking to. Speaking too quickly can make you seem nervous or, with different body language, arrogant, as if you don't have time for the person or people in front of you. Slow down, breathe and *pause*. Pauses give you control, help others process your words and let your message land.

Occasionally people go to the other extreme and speak too slowly. This can convey hesitancy and a lack of confidence, or can simply be boring. If this is your challenge, reflect on what might be causing this and how you can address it. For example, do you need to prepare more fully or build key relationships?

Clarity: Speaking clearly matters, especially in international or multicultural settings where the language you're speaking might not be the first language of all those around you, or your own. Avoid rushing through syllables or slurring words together, especially if you have a strong accent and especially with new people. Once again, people will only ask you to repeat something once or twice at a maximum.

It's easy to get lazy and run words together, or just to use the front of your mouth, which 'flattens' words. Use your full mouth and enunciate words clearly.

Intonation: Without changes in tone, people disengage. Think about what you want to achieve – are you aiming to inspire, impart information or update your listeners? Then consider what tone of voice is appropriate – serious, light-hearted, excited... If you're recounting something, try to imagine it or relive it in your mind as this will naturally improve your intonation.

In some languages, intonation can bring the same phrase to life as a statement, a question or a command. Consider carefully what you are trying to communicate.

You can find a worksheet to help with all these aspects of speaking on my website.[6]

The language of confidence

Once we get beyond the quick first impression of your voice, the words you actually use portray a lot about who you are, your confidence, your credibility and how you engage with others. Confident speakers avoid minimizing phrases like 'Can I just say...?' or 'Sorry, but...', which dilute a message and signal self-doubt.

Similarly, avoid stock phrases like 'To be honest with you...' (what, the rest of the time you aren't being honest?). They're not only meaningless, but they're also often over-used and therefore distract from what you are saying. Value the words you use and avoid 'wasting' any of your airtime.

For the same reason, ditch vague filler words like 'sort of', 'like', 'um', 'to be honest' – these are verbal clutter. It's hard to eradicate them completely, but try to replace them with pauses, which give you time to think about what's next and also give others time to consider what you've said.

Finally, start and end with strength. Too many people deliver a good point... then trail off with 'So yeah, that's it really'. Think about how you'll open and close – even in everyday conversations.

If you're going to speak – especially in a meeting – speak up with clarity, purpose and confidence. If you don't value what you say, why should anyone else? Use your voice intentionally – it's one of the most powerful career tools you have.

✏️ So what? Over to you…

1. When do you find yourself rushing or undermining your message with filler words or nervous energy?

---

2. What's one thing you could do to slow down and be more intentional with your voice in the next important conversation?

3. How could you strengthen how you open and close your contributions in meetings?

Day 5
Managing your time and workload

Time is your most precious resource at work – but how you manage it says a lot about what matters to you, how intentional you are and how much control you have.

If you don't consciously manage your time, time will disappear and you won't be focusing on necessary priorities.

One of the greatest ways to feel more in control and confident is to manage your time proactively and to keep a sense of perspective. It's not necessarily about working longer – it's about being more effective with the time you have.

What to spend your time on (and what NOT to spend your time on…)

Start by thinking carefully about what you spend time on – and whether that truly matters. Not everything urgent is important. Make time for activities that will have longer-term impact such as internal networking, career development, team development and strategic planning.

If you're aiming for promotion, starting to step up and do tasks beyond your role before they fit into your job description is a great way to prove you are ready. It will then make it less of a change when you *are* promoted. If you are finding it challenging to do this, don't be afraid to ask for help and, if relevant, request some training, coaching or mentoring to help you.

You then need to think about prioritizing the different types of tasks and consider the amount of time they each require in a typical week, month or quarter. What percentage of your time *should* they be taking up, and what percentage are they *actually* taking up? You can then make a plan for how to close the gap, if there is one.

Planning your time

Once you know what you're aiming for, a very simple method to help you allocate and track time is to colour-code your diary. Select a colour for each type of task, then apply that to your diary – for both meetings and time you need to spend working on different elements. For example, in my diary client work is purple, client prep and admin are yellow, networking is orange and personal arrangements are green.

This will also help you block out time for the work you need to get done, which is another essential point. If urgent work comes up – which it will – you can just re-jig your diary to find another spot for that work you planned to do. This also means you allocate time for important-but-not-urgent tasks. You could – and many professionals do – entirely fill the day responding to what people are asking from you. But for areas that require more thought and that are more long term, such as strategy or your own career planning, if you don't block out time, nobody else will do it for you.

A good tip is to make sure a day's work is never finished until you have a plan for the next day – what needs to be done (with time blocked out to do it) and what you'll do if you have any extra time. Remember to leave gaps in your day for the unexpected. This might sound obvious, but so few people really plan their working day, and if you do, you'll quickly stand out from the crowd.

Staying visible while managing your load

Visibility matters. If you're excellent but invisible, your contribution may not get recognized. That's especially important when you're working remotely.

Being busy is not the same as being effective – and it's certainly not the same as being *seen* to be effective.

Make sure the right people know what you're working on, where you've added value and how you're contributing. This isn't about bragging, it's about owning your professional narrative.

Time management isn't just about efficiency. It's about self-leadership. How you use your time shows whether you are reacting – or ready for promotion.

✏️ So what? Over to you…

1. What's one activity you know matters but often gets squeezed out of your week?

2. How clear are you with others about your priorities – and how could you be more intentional in communicating them?

3. When you look at your current workload, where are you being busy vs impactful?

Day 6
Building relationships that matter

So far we've looked at what you need to consider for how you show up at work, the things that affect how you are perceived and how you engage with others.

Now we're going to look at the relationships you need and how to build them positively, not only to make your working life more positive and productive and for your own career success, but also for the success of your organization.

Strong working relationships are the invisible driver behind career acceleration. Without them, you can deliver excellent work – and still be overlooked.

The foundations of good relationships are simple: know, like and trust. Let's look at each of these in turn.

Know: Sounds simple, right? People, of course, need to know you to have a relationship with you. Yet so few professional people make the time to know people beyond their obvious day-to-day working environment. Being known at work – in a good way – is essential.

Like: You don't need to bend over backwards and say 'yes' to everything others ask of you. I'm talking about creating a connection with them. You do that simply by being human. Many people are so focused on what they need to achieve or on showcasing what they have been doing that they forget to talk about the weather, ask about someone's family, show that they care about someone as a person.

Trust: Now we're talking. This is the holy grail of work relationships, and this is what's going to get you that promotion. But how do you build it?

Building trust and credibility

We're talking here about more than being trustworthy in everyday life – not running away with someone's laptop bag, for example. We're talking about professional trust, which relates to the degree to which someone believes you are good at your job. Personal trust often comes easily if someone likes you, but professional trust can take more time to develop.

In their book *The Trusted Advisor*, David Maister, Charles Green and Robert Galford identify three elements that increase trust: credibility, reliability and intimacy.[7] Let's consider each of those in turn.

Credibility: People need to be able to believe that you will do a good job. If you're positioning yourself for promotion, those making the decision need to be able to envisage you stepping up into the role. This is closely related to your personal impact, so you're already well positioned to get this right.

Reliability: Doing what you said you would, consistently, is the ultimate trust builder. Sometimes this means managing others' expectations. If you're going to miss a deadline, being reliable would mean warning the relevant people in advance and saying when you expect to meet it. In the long run, this means you will get chased less as people begin to trust you will either deliver or update them if you can't.

Intimacy: In work terms, this simply means connectedness; engaging with people so they feel valued. It means remembering personal details and making time for 'small talk' (which actually isn't small at all, it's all about building rapport so you can have better big conversations).

(Note that Maister, Green and Galford also point out that these three credibility builders can be undercut by 'self-orientation'. If people sense that you're doing these things simply to further your own agenda, then trust will go out of the window.)

People are different

You won't like everyone you encounter at work, and vice versa. But it will help if you keep in mind that people are different. What works with one colleague may not work with another. That's why relationship-building starts with *awareness*, not one-size-fits-all techniques.

Being able to adapt your communication, tone and approach based on others' preferences is a skill – and a career asset.

Top ten relationship skills

Here are ten key skills on which to focus to improve your professional relationships.

1. Consider how you come across

How you come across to others has a huge impact on the way you are perceived and the resulting interactions. Take the time to understand how others could perceive your body language, words and behaviour.

2. Demonstrate empathy

This is an important way to show you value someone and that you have taken the time to share in what they are experiencing – whether that's delight or frustration. Humans want to feel understood, to believe that people 'get us', even if they don't agree with us.

3. Listen

A key way to value others is by remembering what they said, which means listening properly. By listening well you can also avoid misunderstandings and defuse frustration and anger. Instead of thinking what to say next, focus what's being said, asking good questions and taking the time to verify your understanding. This communicates to others that you're confident (even if you don't feel it!).

4. Take the time to react

There's a lot of pressure to react quickly in today's working environment. However, if you read an email quickly and respond quickly after having misinterpreted it, it can set up a negative interaction pattern very quickly. Taking time to react is particularly important when you feel angry or frustrated. Focus on the outcome you want from the situation or relationship. Thinking this through means your reaction is likely to be much better, and if you do go back and do battle, it is likely to land better too, as you're more likely to deliver your message clearly and appropriately.

5. Understand the perspectives of others

Others' frames of reference are very likely to be different from yours. Open questions are a great way to understand where they're coming from without starting with a critique; this approach is also less likely to make someone defensive.

6. Show vulnerability and humility

People are often afraid to appear 'weak' at work but sharing something of yourself with people and showing some vulnerability, when appropriate, can help build positive relationships. When you're willing to say you don't know the answer it reassures people that when you *do* speak, you know what you're talking about. It helps others to be more genuine and transparent too, which means better discussions and improved decision making. Commit to going back to people with the answers they need. People will appreciate your honesty and the time you've taken to get the answer.

7. Appreciate others

Acknowledge others' contributions to make them feel valued. Thank them specifically and/or give credit for work done by others that you are passing on or presenting. (If you are struggling to get credit for work you have done or, worse still, someone else is claiming it, then speak to the person involved, maybe ask whether you can be the one to present the work in a relevant meeting. Don't let people get used to passing off your work as their own.)

8. Establish relationships on the right footing

'Teaching people how to treat you' is a key mantra of *Gravitas* author Caroline Goyder, and it's a vital skill at work.[8] It involves having boundaries: be clear what you will accept and what you won't, and have challenging conversations where you need to. More on this later.

9. Understand how others work

Given that people are different, it's useful to understand the working style of those with whom you work closely, their life pattern and, as far as you can, their stresses and strains. If someone's not a morning person, don't hit them with a big issue first thing. Agreeing how and when you communicate with those around you will enable you to work together.

10. Establish positive communication patterns

Regular, defined catch-ups are an important part of relationship-building – consider who you should be meeting with, online or offline, and how often. Communication needs to be more intentional in a hybrid or virtual work setting. Think about which communication method is best based on the situation and what you know about the preferences of the other person. Some people are happy for you to just call them and check whether they have five minutes to spare, while others prefer an email to arrange something.

These skills aren't 'soft' – they're *strategic*. As your career progresses, your success increasingly depends on how well you engage and influence others.

So what? Over to you…

1. Who are the three most strategically important people you need stronger relationships with right now?

2. What do those people value – and how could you show up more effectively in their world?

3. Which of the ten relationship skills could you focus on improving over the coming week?

Day 7

Standing out in meetings

We spend a huge proportion of our working lives in meetings – nearly 23 days per year, with 13 of those reportedly unproductive. Research from *Harvard Business Review* found that 71% of senior managers considered meetings to be inefficient.[9] Unproductive meetings not only waste time but also lead to longer working hours and frustration.

However, meetings present powerful opportunities to shape perceptions, build relationships and be seen. It's easy to fall into the trap of being a passive participant, but visibility in meetings often correlates with career impact. Meetings are where decisions are made, perspectives are heard and impressions are formed.

How to prepare and contribute effectively

You can't always choose which meetings to attend, but you can influence what you get from them and how you're perceived. First, know the meeting's purpose. Is it to make a decision? Brainstorm ideas? Share updates? If this isn't clear from the invitation, ask. Clarifying the aim sets expectations and enables better contributions.

Where possible, prepare. This might include reading material in advance, making notes about key points you'd like to raise or checking in with stakeholders beforehand. In some cases, speaking to someone before the meeting to share an idea can mean they support it during the session, increasing its impact. A word of caution, though: you'll never be able to plan for every eventuality. If you get asked a tricky question, remember that 'I don't know but I'll find out and get back to you' is a perfectly reasonable answer!

Speaking up with confidence

Not being visible – or audible – in key meetings can hamper career progression. You don't want to end up speaking simply for the sake of saying something, so consider beforehand what you can contribute that is valuable. But no matter how well prepared you are, speaking up in meetings can feel daunting. Many people fear they'll be judged or that their ideas won't land well. Yet the more you speak, the easier it becomes – and the more you'll be perceived as someone with leadership potential.

If you're not in the habit of speaking up, you may need to signal your intention to contribute when the moment is right. Use your body language: move forward, lean in and gesticulate. If it looks like a point is coming to an end and moving on and you still have something to say, then it's acceptable to interrupt with something like, 'Can I add, before we move on...?'

If someone interrupts you mid-flow, say you'd like to finish and carry on – remember, 'teach people how to treat you.' If you refer back to someone who's tried to interrupt you once you've finished, that shows respect the other way and people will be less likely to interrupt you in the future.

Meetings can be a great way to build your visibility with more senior people, and to build a perception of you and your personal brand, so it is worth considering how you want and need to come across. It's also useful to ask your line manager whether you can attend other meetings that might be useful for visibility. (Likewise, if you manage others, think about opportunities for them to step up and gain more exposure and experience.)

Virtual meetings pose their own challenges, and you need to think about how others will see you. Position your camera to show your shoulders and hands when gesturing. Avoid sitting too far back or too close. Wear colours that contrast well with your background and ensure your space is distraction-free. In virtual settings, a strong presence can help others take notice.

When leading meetings, make them purposeful. Invite only those who need to be there. Clearly state the objectives, stick to the agenda and summarize next steps at the end. Afterwards, follow up with a concise recap and ensure actions are allocated.

Meetings are more than calendar-fillers. They're stages on which your personal impact, ideas and presence are on display. Being deliberate about how you engage in them can significantly change how you are perceived – and remembered.

So what? Over to you...

1. How could you prepare more effectively for meetings to increase your impact?

2. What behaviours would help you speak up more confidently – in person or virtually?

3. Which meetings or presentation opportunities could you proactively seek out?

Day 8
Handling difficult conversations

Most career challenges involve other people. Whether it's difficult colleagues, feedback you're unsure how to handle or tension that hasn't been resolved, these situations are common – and they matter. Here are ten key principles to keep in mind to help you manage these conversations better and avoid damaging your promotion prospects.

1. **Establish** how the other person or people involved have made you feel and consider whether that was really the intention. There could be any number of reasons why someone said or did something that made you feel slighted, but you won't know unless you have

another, empathetic and open, conversation. Similarly, you might react defensively to criticism in a way that clouds your ability to see what the other person could be seeing – be aware of this.

2. **Make proper time for difficult conversations**. Arrange a meeting to discuss the situation properly rather than tacking it on to or hijacking another meeting.

3. **Consider your role in a difficult situation**. Thinking about how your behaviours or actions might have contributed to the situation will help you approach the conversation with greater humility and prepare you for what the other person might bring up.

4. **Avoid blame attribution**. It's rare that all the blame is on you or the other party. The reality is usually somewhere in between.

5. **Listening is a key skill**. Making sure both of you feel heard will help you to move forward together to work on resolving the issue. Paraphrasing and checking your understanding are helpful ways to make sure you're clear and that the other person feels valued.

6. **Avoid dressing up bad news**. In general, don't try to sweeten things. It's better to be

upfront about what you want to discuss in factual language while showing empathy and acknowledging your own feelings.

7. **Extrapolating a situation to make a judgement.** Avoid labels (e.g. 'selfish') and focus on the issue itself. A useful phrase is 'How would you feel in my situation/from my perspective?'

8. **Staying calm is key.** Otherwise, the other person is likely to be responding to your emotional state rather than the facts of the situation. Focus on the key areas that need discussing rather than expressing all your frustrations.

9. **Check any assumptions you have.** It can skew the conversation if the other person has completely different assumptions. What makes complete sense to you may look very different to someone else with a different perspective.

10. **Be open to being persuaded.** This is important if you are truly going to problem solve with the other person. It's also worth asking them what might persuade them to have a different view or position. Being open and a little vulnerable is most likely to help

you reach a good outcome as it will encourage
the other person to be open too.

Taking an initial step in these conversations is hard,
but with time, your relationships will improve if
you tackle what needs to be discussed. As we saw
previously, the more effort you put into building these
relationships at the start, the easier these challenging
conversations will be.

Navigating office politics

Office politics often has negative connotations:
gossip, cliques and favouritism. But politics is simply
the reality of different people with different values,
assumptions and working styles navigating the
same space. It becomes toxic when people withhold
information, speak in whispers or avoid conflict
altogether.

Everyone plays a role – including you. It's
tempting to see others as political while perceiving
yourself as neutral, but how do others view you?

Difficult dynamics often begin with a
misunderstanding. Consider this example: a colleague
regularly dominates meetings. One day they present
on a topic your manager usually leads. You see this
as attention-seeking. In reality, your manager asked

them to do it – but didn't tell you. From now on, you are wary of this person, feeling they are always trying to look better than you – even though this may not be their objective at all. However, this can affect how you behave towards them, which they then react to. This is an example of how negative cycles start.

To halt negative spirals, start with yourself. How are you reacting? How might you approach the person differently? Even small shifts in behaviour can reset the dynamic.

You must be savvy about what is going on around you but avoid jumping to conclusions. Being as transparent as you can be in your communication will help others be the same in theirs. You can't change others' behaviour except by changing your own. Those who avoid learning how to navigate office politics typically stunt their progression.

The right level of detail

At work, it's easy to over-explain or under-share. When dealing with senior colleagues, too much detail can make you appear bogged down or unable to think strategically. Too little, and it may seem like you're glossing over key facts. Learn what different people need and flex accordingly.

This is a key issue if you're aiming for promotion, as one reason why people often don't get promoted is that senior people fear a level of detail will be lost once you have moved on from that role. Consider this: are you too far into the detail and sharing too much? If you appear bogged down in detail, it's hard to be perceived as someone who is ready to step up. People will not only draw the conclusion that it would be a challenge to lose you from the current role, but also that you are less capable of seeing the big picture – a vital skill at more senior levels.

Always consider carefully what your audience really needs to know, and who really needs to be involved. Too many people in a discussion can dramatically impact effectiveness.

Disagreements and difficult conversations are not just inevitable – they are critical to progress. Being willing to engage with care, curiosity and confidence sets you apart as someone ready for leadership.

So what? Over to you…

1. What challenging relationship or pattern at
    work needs your attention right now?

2. How could you approach a difficult conversation with greater confidence and calm?

3. What's one behaviour you could change this
   week to improve a tense dynamic?

Day 9

Increasing your visibility
and influence

Your professional reputation is critical to your career progression. You can be highly capable, but if no one knows about it, you may be overlooked.

Visibility isn't about self-promotion for its own sake – it's about making sure the right people are aware of your value.

Building a strong professional reputation

Delivering results is essential – but so is how you work with others. Consistency, reliability and constructive engagement all build reputation over time.

Positive visibility means being seen as someone who adds value – someone others want to work with.

You don't want to be known just for the work you deliver, but for the way you deliver it. That includes collaboration, responsiveness and problem-solving skills.

Think about how others experience you daily. Are you visible to key people? If not, what could you do to raise your professional profile in ways that feel authentic? We've already looked at speaking up in meetings (see Day 7 if you want a reminder). Here are a few more visibility opportunities to consider.

Presenting

Whether it's presenting information in a low-key way from your seat in a meeting or presenting on a stage at a conference, being willing and able to present engagingly and confidently is one of the best skills you can develop to build your visibility. People who are unwilling or unable to do this well hold back their progression.

Yes, it can be scary. A little fear can be good – it gets the adrenaline going. But there's no need to be paralyzed by fear. People want you to do well and most of the time they want to hear what you have to say as it might be useful, helpful or even necessary to them.

Remember that although what you are presenting may feel like 'old knowledge' to you, for the most part it is 'new' to the audience, so value it and speak slowly and clearly with positive body language. Wherever possible, you want to take your audience on a journey with you; storytelling is a powerful way to get engagement and to help the audience remember what you said.

If you're not used to presenting, look out for even tiny opportunities to present information. Start small and work up; consider internal and external options. Some people find it easier presenting to new people rather than colleagues.

Here are my top tips for presenting (and you can find a presentation skills sheet on my website to help).[10]

1. Think carefully about your audience

Who are they? Why do they want to hear this material? Knowing this will help you frame your message. If you aren't clear on what you want to communicate and why, the audience won't be either.

2. Supporting materials

A slide deck can be useful but it's not essential, and it definitely shouldn't work without you! Don't write your script on the slides, use them as a prompt for what you want to say, and don't talk to the screen or your audience will quickly switch off.

3. Notes and scripts

Unless you're presenting a formal speech at a lectern, scripts are a no-no. Just know what you want to say (and don't memorize it word for word either!) and, if it helps, use prompt cards with single words on them to remind you, or if you're using PowerPoint, let your slides be your prompt. Your words will be so much more engaging than if you were reading them.

4. Body language

This is key for communicating confidence and engaging others. Own your space, look at the audience and be deliberate with your hand gestures. Having a clicker in one hand can help a lot if you are standing to present PowerPoint slides! There is almost always one very smiley, reassuring person in the audience. Locate that person early on and, when you are doubting yourself, look at them – but don't stare!

Great presentations don't just happen, they take planning and thought. How you deliver is at least as important as what you present. If you don't keep people engaged, they won't take the message on board anyway! The more you present, the easier it will become and the better you will get at it, so think about how you can improve from where you are at now.

Making the most of your online presence

The internet extends your professional footprint beyond the people you meet day-to-day. That can be tricky. If you have never done it before, it's worth bringing up an incognito web browser window and searching your name to check what is freely available online about you. Are there any photos of you online you *wouldn't* want to be visible to your senior leadership team? Is there anything that contradicts your personal brand and the perception you want to create? If so, and if you can, fix that first; make sure, for example, that personal photos and comments are 'friends only'.

(I have a policy of not being 'friends' on social media with people I know professionally. Someone who's a peer at work now might one day be your boss – or you could be theirs – and you might not want them to have access to personal information.)

Of all the online platforms, LinkedIn in particular is critical for professional visibility, credibility and personal brand. It's not just used by recruiters. Internal colleagues often look people up before a first meeting, and they'll think it strange if they can't find you on there.

Your LinkedIn profile

If you haven't built much of a profile on LinkedIn until now, it is worth allocating two to three hours to work on it. If you do that well, then a check every few months should be sufficient to update it with anything new. It shouldn't just be about job changes.

Top tip: before you make any updates, change the settings so that every change isn't visible to your network. You may want to change this back just before you make the final change so that your network is encouraged to view your profile.

It's worth optimizing your profile for two key reasons:

1. So people are encouraged to read it and feel it reinforces the person they know, if they know you in real life; and
2. So it appears in searches. This is key when you are looking for a new role.

When it comes to showing up in searches, LinkedIn algorithms reward you for being active on the platform, having 500+ connections (at the time of writing) and having a fairly complete profile with appropriate key words.

Here are the key things to think about as you set up or review your LinkedIn profile.

1. **A photo that looks like you now** so people can find you quickly if they have met you before, especially if you have a common name. This photo needs to be appropriate for your job role and represent your personal brand positively.
2. **A banner image at the top**. This can be something related to the area in which you work or your location, or even something more personal (with care). Check that it works well on the app version of the platform too.

3. **Headline**. A job title is useful but dull: add a little more about what you do (e.g. not just 'family law solicitor', but also 'helping families resolve their disputes quickly').

4. **'About' section**. This is an opportunity to say a bit more about yourself: what you have achieved, what you enjoy, what your expertise is and how you help those you serve – whether internal or external clients.

5. **Experience section**. Don't just make this a CV or list of job titles, add something about your responsibilities and achievements in each role.

6. **Education**. If you've been working for 20 years and have a degree, don't include your school qualifications. There are additional sections you can add for courses, awards, and so on, so consider where you want different elements to feature.

7. **Skills**. A good way to showcase what you are good at and, again, to guide searches.

8. **Recommendations**. This is an opportunity for people to understand more about what you do and what it's like to work with you. You may need to give people a structure to follow for their recommendation to increase

the chance of them completing it – such as why/in what situation you worked together, what you did, what you were like to work with and the outcome.

9. **Additional elements**. You can add many different sections, so if you have been a volunteer or contributed to publications, consider what you want to feature and where it best sits. You don't have to get too personal, but LinkedIn does give you an opportunity to show some of your personality and build your brand.

If you complete these sections well, you will be on your way to a great profile. You can find a useful LinkedIn profile checklist on my website.[11]

Building your visibility on LinkedIn

LinkedIn can be your professional contacts address book if you are diligent about connecting with others – which means connecting with everyone you meet in real life, whether in person or virtually, such as at meetings or at a networking event.

When you set up your profile invite people you know professionally as well as appropriate personal contacts, and as you build your network, make time to interact with your connections. That might be as simple as hitting an appropriate emoticon (always make sure you read the post fully first!), but it can be more thoughtful:

- **Commenting** is a great way to show engagement and knowledge, or to share an opinion, and can help those outside your immediate network to become aware of you; the connections of the person whose post you commented on may see your comment, particularly if they have also engaged with the post.
- **Sharing** when something is useful or interesting for your network. Always add a comment to introduce what you are sharing and why. You can also send posts to specific contacts via a message.
- **Creating your own content** such as a post, a poll or an article, for example.
- **Searching for relevant contacts and connections**. As long as you aren't pushy, you may be surprised by how open most people are to connecting. Again, always include a message.

LinkedIn regularly updates the platform, so stay on top of these to keep your profile and visibility up to date.

Who you accept connection requests from is ultimately your choice. I tend to accept anyone from industries that are in some way related to my work. If they haven't sent a message, I send them one asking what prompted them to connect with me. I am often positively surprised by the response, and this can start an interesting conversation.

The degree to which you interact on LinkedIn will depend on what your aim is, but no matter what your situation, plan to be visible regularly. After all, the senior managers in your company will be searching for likely candidates when a vacancy comes up, and they might as well see you first!

So what? Over to you...

1. How visible are you right now to the people
    who matter for your career goals?

2. Where are you at with speaking in meetings and/or presenting? How could you step this up?

3. Is your LinkedIn profile/activity representing you at your best?

Day 10
Preparing for promotion

Promotion isn't just about technical skills – it's about readiness to operate at a higher level. That means ensuring that senior leaders are aware of you and perceive you to be capable of making the step up, and THAT means you need to be careful about the level of detail at which you currently operate, and therefore what others associate you with. You may need to delegate more and train up potential successors so your manager feels more comfortable about losing you from your current role!

When you've put all that in place, built the right strategic relationships internally and worked on the skills you need that we've outlined in this book, internal promotion is far more likely to happen.

Assessing your readiness

Before you pursue promotion, be honest with yourself. Are you already operating at the level you're aiming for? If not, what gaps need closing?

Think about technical skills, yes, but also about leadership, strategic thinking, communication and influencing skills.

Sometimes it's not a lack of skill that holds people back – it's a lack of visibility or a lack of trust that they can step up.

Wanting a promotion is rarely just about a better salary and package, although that might be the surface reason. It's usually related to unfulfilling work, feeling under-appreciated (usually related to poor relationships) or a lack of work–life balance.

For some people, a role change is the right move, but for many, changes in your current working patterns, skills and habits can dramatically improve how you feel about your work.

My best advice is to make some time to really think about what is and isn't going well at work. Then you can get a sense of whether smaller changes within your current career – such as moving organization or even department, upskilling and/or working on your relationships and non-technical skills – could shift the situation.

You could do that work on your own, with the help of a trusted friend/colleague or with a career expert. I'd advise you to not rush into making a big change (it's easy to think things are better elsewhere) and to make some time for quality thinking.

Making your case

If you want a promotion, you need to make a strong business case.

Prepare tangible examples of where you've delivered impact, taken ownership, led initiatives and contributed beyond your formal role.

Frame your request not as entitlement, but as readiness to add more value.

Consider your rationale carefully. Stay factual and confident.

Promotion conversations can feel personal, but framing them around business value helps keep them professional and persuasive.

The interview mindset

Even internal promotions often require a formal interview. Treat it seriously.

Many people feel daunted by an interview – thinking of it as a conversation can help. You need to be right for the role, but the role also needs to be right for you – it isn't a one-sided transaction.

When you attend an interview, there are three key aspects to keep in mind: the content of your answers, the impact you have on the interviewer(s) and the rapport you build.

Be clear about why you want the role and be able to demonstrate this credibly through knowledge about the company and the role while relating this to your own experience and skills.

In answering the questions, always consider what the interviewer really wants to know and how you can best showcase your skills and experience. A helpful framework for the examples you give is the CAR framework: a bit of *Context* so the person knows what was happening and ideally how challenging a situation was, followed by the *Action* you personally took – what you did and the skills you demonstrated – and concluding with the *Result*.

Even if you are asked something where you provide a conceptual answer or some principles you would apply, try to support this with an example to show you have actually done this. If you haven't, take a similar example and adapt it to illustrate how you think and how you approach situations and challenges.

After you have been asked a question, it is absolutely fine to take a few seconds to consider your answer. You can even vocalize now and then that you are thinking about the best example or response to give. Most of all, make sure you answer the question you are asked, not the one you think you heard!

Asking some questions at the end helps to show your interest. One of these could be about the next steps in the decision-making process, if you are successful, as well as the culture of the team and its key challenges, if the role is in a different team.

If you are not successful at interview, then try to get as much feedback as possible, as this will help you improve for the next opportunity.

By preparing carefully – and approaching promotion as a strategic project – you significantly increase your chances of success.

So what? Over to you…

1. If you were your own manager, would you promote yourself today? Why or why not?

2. What concrete examples can you use to demonstrate your readiness for the next step?

3. How could you strengthen your visibility and case for promotion over the next three months?

Conclusion

Wherever you are in your career, the skills and strategies you've explored in this book can help you take control of your progress and your fulfilment at work.

The journey isn't about perfection. It's about awareness, action and adjustment.

Professional success isn't just about technical expertise. It's about personal impact, relationship-building, communication and strategic visibility.

Remember, others can support you, but your career is ultimately yours to drive.

By applying what you've explored here – step by step, situation by situation – you'll be better equipped to navigate challenges, seize opportunities and build the career you truly want.

Take ownership. Take action. And get that promotion!

Endnotes

1 A. Todorov and J. Willis, *First Impressions: Making Up Your Mind After a 100-Ms Exposure to a Face* (2005).

2 J. Neffinger and M. Kohut, *Compelling People: The Hidden Qualities That Make Us Influential* (2014).

3 See https://insideoutimage.co.uk/articles/book-resource-2-personal-brand

4 M. L. Damhorst, 'In search of a common thread: Classification of information communicated through dress' in *Clothing and Textiles Research Journal*, 8 (2), 1–12 (1990).

5 See https://insideoutimage.co.uk/articles/book-resource-4-body-language

6 See https://insideoutimage.co.uk/articles/book-resource-5-voice-elements

7 D. H. Maister, C. H. Green and R. M. Galford, *The Trusted Advisor*, 20th anniversary edition (2021).

8 C. Goyder, *Gravitas: Communicate with Confidence, Influence and Authority* (2014).

9 L.A. Perlow, C.N. Hadley and E. Eun, 'Stop the meeting madness', *Harvard Business Review*, July–August 2017, https://hbr.org/2017/07/stop-the-meeting-madness [accessed 13 August 2025].

10 See https://insideoutimage.co.uk/articles/book-resource-17-presentation-skills

11 See https://insideoutimage.co.uk/articles/book-resource-14-linkedin-profile

Enjoyed this?
Then you'll love…

Getting On: Making Work Work by Joanna Gaudoin

You've come this far… How do you move your career forward from here?

Once you reach middle to senior level in your profession, you require different skills to allow you not only to carry out your day-to-day role effectively and positively, but also to continue your career progression and fulfil your potential. Simply being technically proficient and having expert knowledge isn't enough anymore. You need to develop other capabilities related to communicating, engaging with others and dealing with every professional scenario effectively and confidently. This book will help you master these skills to successfully navigate your current role and prepare for your next one, so that you can increase your job satisfaction and progress your career.

Joanna Gaudoin helps bright, knowledgeable people with great technical skills and experience improve their non-technical skills, so they progress their careers and boost their firm's performance. She has run her business for over a decade and has worked with thousands of people, both individually and in groups. Now she wants to help YOU stand out and develop the skills you need to succeed.

Other 6-Minute Smarts titles

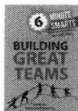

Building Great Teams (based on *Workshop Culture* by Alison Coward)

Collaborate Better (based on *Collabor(h)ate* by Deb Mashek PhD)

Customer Success Essentials (based on *The Customer Success Pioneer* by Kellie Lucas)

Do Change Better (based on *How to be a Change Superhero* by Lucinda Carney)

Find Your Confidence (based on *Coach Yourself Confident* by Julie Smith)

How to be Happy at Work (based on *My Job Isn't Working!* by Michael Brown)

Sales Made Simple (based on *More Sales Please* by Sara Nasser Dalrymple)

The Speed Storytelling Toolkit (based on *Exposure* by Felicity Cowie)

Stay Focused (based on *Attention!* by Rob Hatch)

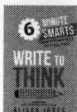

Write to Think (based on *Exploratory Writing* by Alison Jones)

Look out for more titles coming soon! Visit www.practicalinspiration.com for all our latest titles.